To Be Continued...

1930'S & 1940'S SERIAL MOVIE POSTERS

volume sixteen of
the illustrated history of movies through posters

Previous Volumes:
Volume One: Cartoon Movie Posters
Volume Two: Cowboy Movie Posters
Volume Three: Academy Award® Winners' Movie Posters
Volume Four: Sports Movie Posters
Volume Five: Crime Movie Posters
Volume Six: More Cowboy Movie Posters
Volume Seven: Horror Movie Posters
Volume Eight: Best Pictures' Movie Posters
Volume Nine: Musical Movie Posters
Volume Ten: Serial Movie Posters
Volume Eleven: Horror, Sci-Fi & Fantasy Movie Posters
Volume Twelve: Comedy Movie Posters
Volume Thirteen: War Movie Posters
Volume Fourteen: Attack of the "B" Movie Posters
Volume Fifteen: Not Nominated Movie Posters

Edited and published by Bruce Hershenson
Published by Bruce Hershenson
P.O. Box 874, West Plains, MO 65775
Phone: (417) 256-9616 Fax: (417) 257-6948
mail@brucehershenson.com (e-mail)
http://www.brucehershenson.com or
http://www.emovieposter.com (website)

IF YOU ENJOYED THIS MOVIE POSTER BOOK, THEN YOU ARE SURE TO ENJOY THESE OTHER SIMILAR BRUCE HERSHENSON PUBLICATIONS. LOOK FOR THEM AT YOUR LOCAL BOOKSTORE OR ORDER THEM DIRECT FROM THE PUBLISHER.

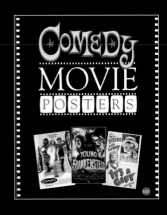

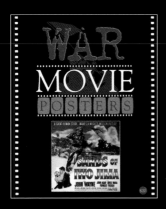

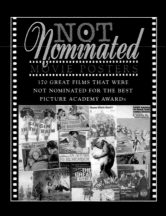

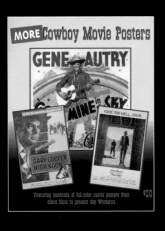

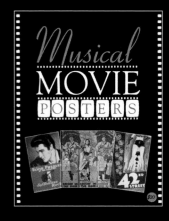

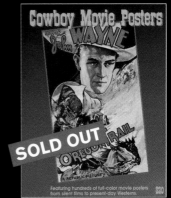

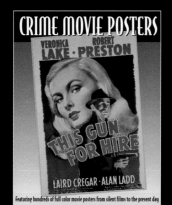

Introduction

Welcome to the sixteenth volume of the Illustrated History of Movies Through Posters. This book is different from the previous volumes in an unusual way. Almost all of the images in the previous volumes came from the archive I co-own with my partner, Richard Allen, the Hershenson-Allen Archive (the archive consists of over 35,000 different movie poster images, all photographed directly from the original posters onto high quality 4"x 5"color transparencies; There is not another resource like it anywhere, and it is the world's foremost source of movie poster images).

But almost all of the posters in this volume came from a most unusual collection. Let me explain. In 1939, eight year old Frank Gutierrez (and his younger sister Roberta) were growing up in San Francisco. Fate led them to the street in the city where the movie poster exchanges were located. Frank went into the Republic Pictures Exchange, and persuaded the man there to sell him a brand-new one-sheet poster for a current serial, which Frank had seen in a theater. The price was fifteen cents! Over the next six years Frank accumulated well over 100 posters from serial films of the 1930s and early 1940s. As he grew older he developed other interests, and he stopped seeking out posters, but unlike the vast majority of collectors who give away or throw out their childhood collections, he kept all of his posters. In the 1960s Frank discovered collectible shops and shows, and he searched for titles to add to his collection, but he quickly saw that, even in the 1960s, posters from serial films were extremely rare.

Why was that so? One likely reason is that most theaters in the 1930s and 1940s only showed single chapters of serials at their Saturday Matinees, along with a double feature and some cartoons (to see the complete serial the kids would have to return week after week). They probably felt there was little need to buy a poster advertising the single chapter of a serial they were showing on a particular day. Whether there was much of a demand or not, the studios would make one-sheets for every chapter of each serial, each of which usually had a large photo inset that would show a duotone scene from that chapter. But they would also usually make posters that advertised the entire serial and these would usually be elaborate full-color artwork posters (Those films that didn't have separate posters for the entire serial usually had full artwork Chapter One posters). Quite naturally these posters are much more rare and desirable than those for the individual chapters.

Frank Gutierrez sought out the full artwork posters whenever he could find them, and over two-thirds of the serial films represented in this volume include a poster either for the entire serial (or from the first chapter). There is not another collection of serial posters to equal this one anywhere in the world!

I need to thank Phillip Wages, Erik Bennett, Sean Burke, and Sylvia Hershenson, who assisted in the preparation and proofreading of this book. I also need to thank Amy Knight who did the layouts and designed the covers.

I dedicate this book to Frank Gutierrez and all the other early pioneers of movie poster collecting. I am happiest that Frank has been able to see that so many others now recognize what he has known for many years; that movie posters are not disposable advertising, but are a true American art form!

Bruce Hershenson
June 2001

To Be Continued... INDEX

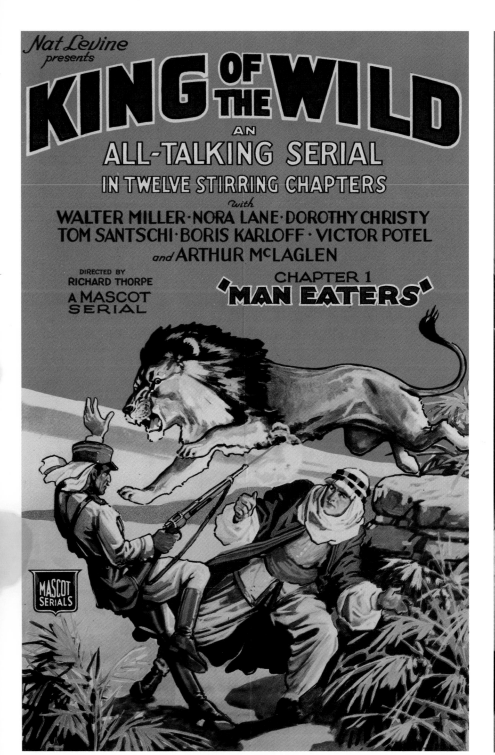

1. KING OF THE WILD,
Chapter 1, 1931, one-sheet

2. KING OF THE WILD,
Chapter 2, 1931, one-sheet

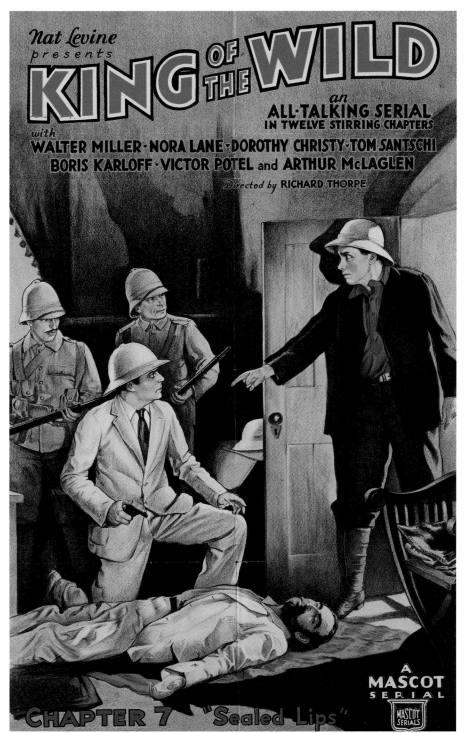

3. KING OF THE WILD,
Chapter 7, 1931, one-sheet

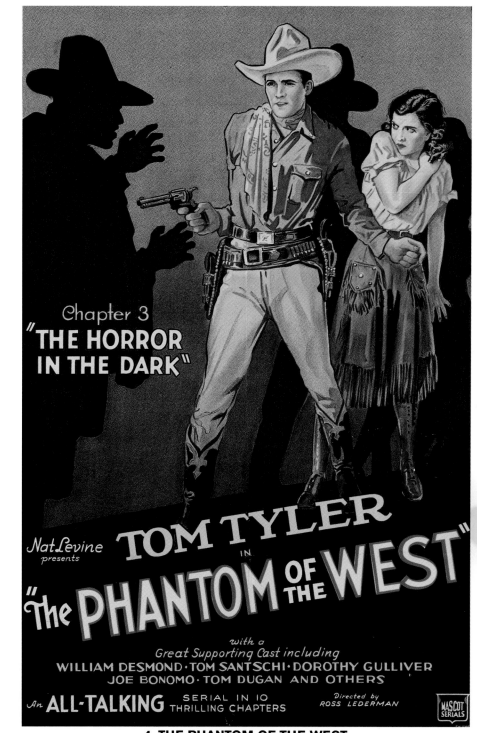

4. THE PHANTOM OF THE WEST,
Chapter 3, 1931, one-sheet

5. THE GALLOPING GHOST,
entire serial, 1931 (1937 reissue), one-sheet

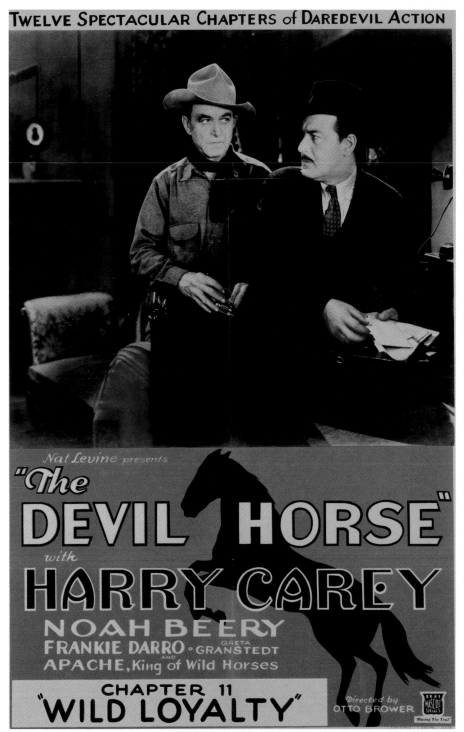

6. THE DEVIL HORSE,
Chapter 11, 1932, one-sheet

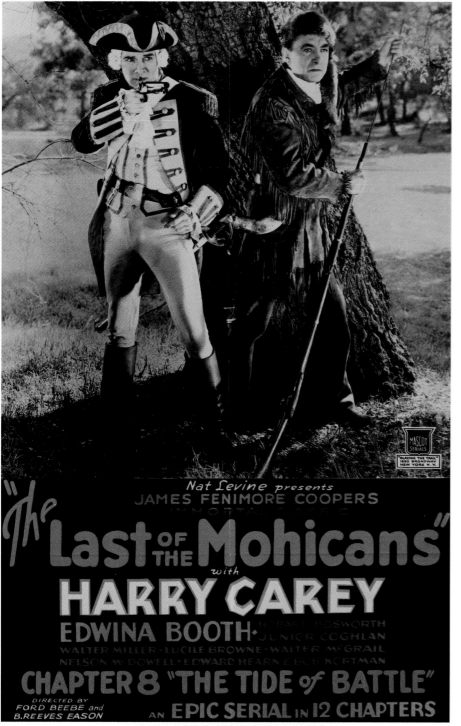

7. THE LAST OF THE MOHICANS,
Chapter 8, 1932, one-sheet

8. THE LAST OF THE MOHICANS,
Chapter 11, 1932, one-sheet

9. TARZAN THE FEARLESS,
Chapter 1, 1933, one-sheet

10. TARZAN THE FEARLESS,
Chapter 3, 1933, one-sheet

11. TARZAN THE FEARLESS,
Chapter 5, 1933, one-sheet

12. TARZAN THE FEARLESS,
feature version, 1933, one-sheet

13. TARZAN THE FEARLESS,
entire serial, banner, 1933

14. THE RED RIDER,
entire serial, banner, 1934

15. GORDON OF GHOST CITY,
entire serial, 1933, one-sheet

16. MYSTERY MOUNTAIN,
Chapter 7, 1934, one-sheet

17. THE RETURN OF CHANDU,
Chapter 11, 1934, one-sheet

18. THE LOST JUNGLE,
Chapter 4, 1934, one-sheet

19. LAW OF THE WILD,
Chapter 12, 1934, one-sheet

20. THE ADVENTURES OF REX AND RINTY,
Chapter 2, 1935, one-sheet

21. THE FIGHTING MARINES,
entire serial, 1935, one-sheet

22. THE FIGHTING MARINES,
Chapter 4, 1935, one-sheet

23. THE PHANTOM EMPIRE,
1935 (1940's reissue), one-sheet

24. THE LOST CITY,
Chapter 10, 1935, one-sheet

25. THE NEW ADVENTURES OF TARZAN,
Style A feature version, 1935, one-sheet

26. THE NEW ADVENTURES OF TARZAN,
Style B feature version, 1935, one-sheet

27. THE NEW ADVENTURES OF TARZAN,
Chapter 2, 1935, one-sheet

28. FLASH GORDON,
Chapter 4, 1936, one-sheet

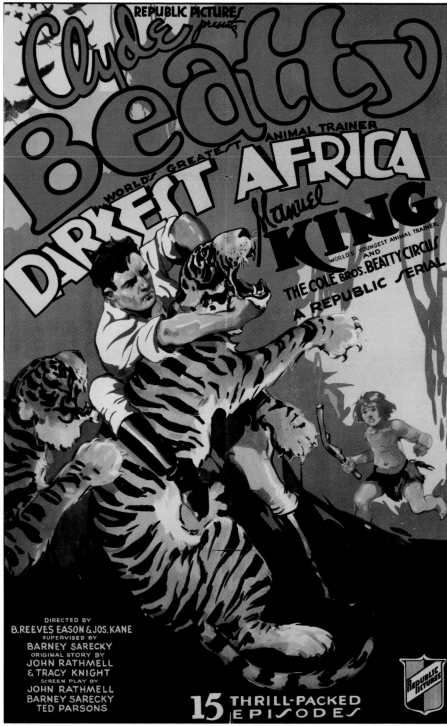

29. DARKEST AFRICA,
entire serial, 1936, one-sheet

30. DARKEST AFRICA,
Chapter 1, 1936, one-sheet

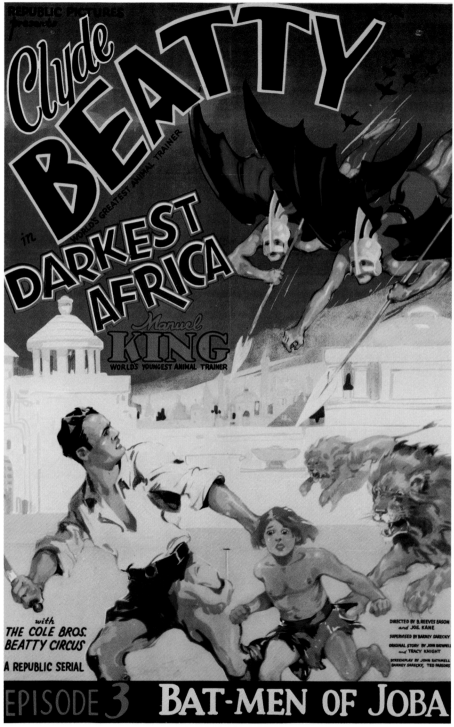

31. DARKEST AFRICA,
Chapter 3, 1936, one-sheet

32. DARKEST AFRICA,
Chapter 4, 1936, one-sheet

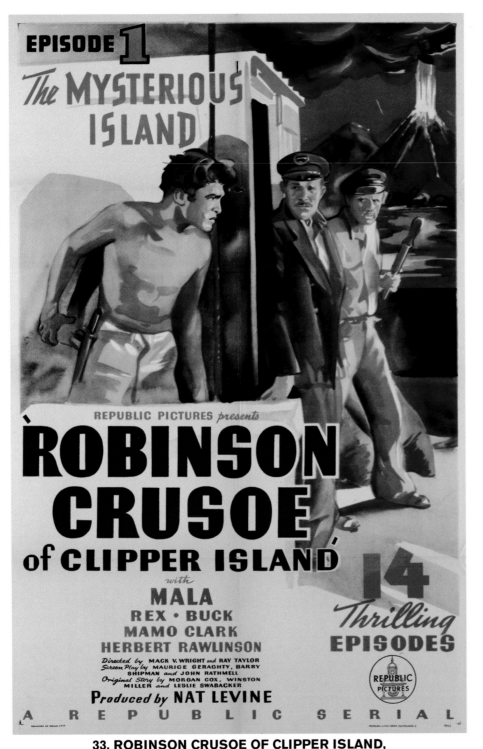

33. ROBINSON CRUSOE OF CLIPPER ISLAND,
Chapter 1, 1936, one-sheet

34. ROBINSON CRUSOE OF CLIPPER ISLAND,
Chapter 2, 1936, one-sheet

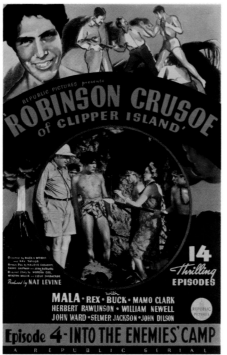

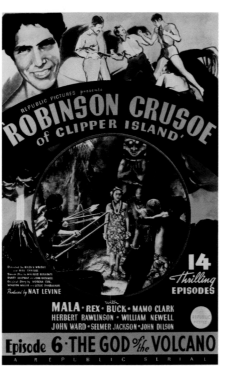

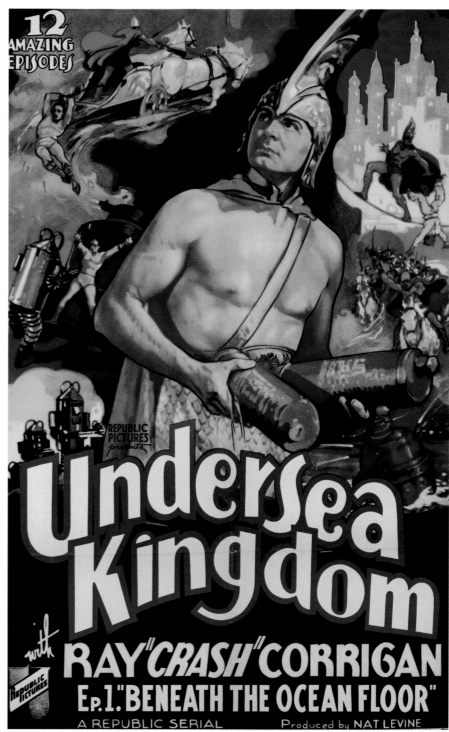

35-38. ROBINSON CRUSOE OF CLIPPER ISLAND,
Chapters 3, 4, 5, 6 1936, one-sheets

39. UNDERSEA KINGDOM,
Chapter 1, 1936, one-sheet

40. THE VIGILANTES ARE COMING,
Chapter 1, 1936, one-sheet

41. THE VIGILANTES ARE COMING,
Chapter 5, 1936, one-sheet

42. BLAKE OF SCOTLAND YARD,
entire serial, 1937, one-sheet

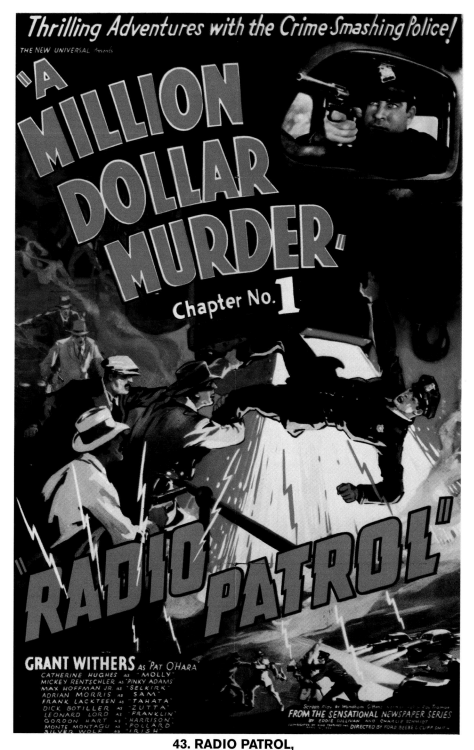

43. RADIO PATROL,
Chapter 1, 1937, one-sheet

44. DICK TRACY,
Chapter 1, 1937, one-sheet

45. DICK TRACY,
Chapter 2, 1937, one-sheet

46. WILD WEST DAYS,
Chapter 4, 1937, one-sheet

47. THE PAINTED STALLION,
Chapter 4, 1937, one-sheet

48. TIM TYLER'S LUCK,
Chapter 1, 1937, one-sheet

49. ZORRO RIDES AGAIN,
Chapter 3, 1937, one-sheet

50. S.O.S. COAST GUARD,
Chapter 10, 1937, one-sheet

51. DICK TRACY RETURNS,
Chapter 5, 1938, one-sheet

52. FLASH GORDON'S TRIP TO MARS,
entire serial, 1938, one-sheet

53. FLASH GORDON'S TRIP TO MARS,
Chapter 6, 1938, one-sheet

54. FLASH GORDON'S TRIP TO MARS,
Chapter 14, 1938, one-sheet

55. RED BARRY,
Chapter 1, 1938, one-sheet

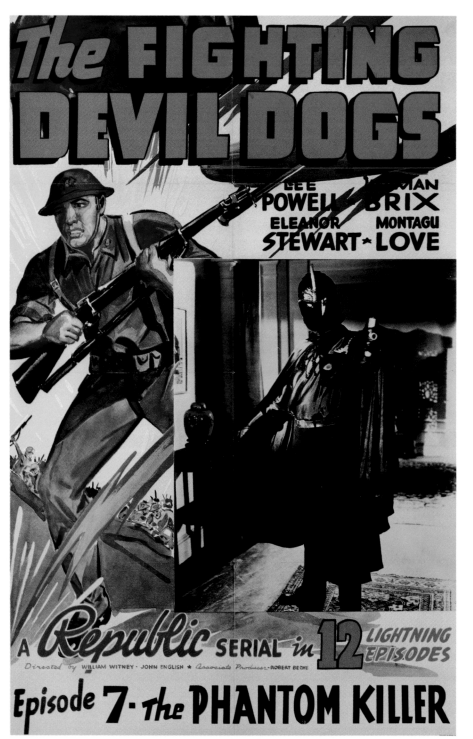

56. THE FIGHTING DEVIL DOGS,
Chapter 7, 1938, one-sheet

57. THE FIGHTING DEVIL DOGS,
Feature Version, 1938, one-sheet

58. FLAMING FRONTIERS,
Chapter 11, 1938, one-sheet

59. THE LONE RANGER,
Chapter 2, 1938, one-sheet

60. HAWK OF THE WILDERNESS,
Chapter 4, 1938, one-sheet

61. DAREDEVILS OF THE RED CIRCLE,
Chapter 3, 1939, one-sheet

62. THE PHANTOM CREEPS,
entire serial, 1939, one-sheet

63. DICK TRACY'S G-MEN,
Chapter 15, 1939, one-sheet

64. THE GREEN HORNET STRIKES AGAIN!,
Chapter 9, one-sheet

65. MYSTERIOUS DOCTOR SATAN,
Chapter 5, 1940, one-sheet

66. ADVENTURES OF RED RYDER,
Chapter 1, 1940, one-sheet

67. ADVENTURES OF RED RYDER,
Chapter 12, 1940, one-sheet

68. FLASH GORDON CONQUERS THE UNIVERSE,
entire serial, 1940, one-sheet

69. BUCK ROGERS,
entire serial, 1940, one-sheet

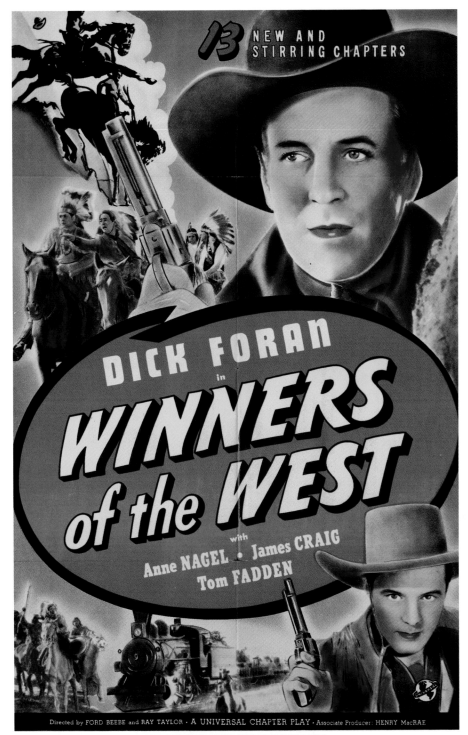

70. WINNERS OF THE WEST,
entire serial, 1940, one-sheet

71. KING OF THE ROYAL MOUNTED,
Chapter 1, 1940, one-sheet

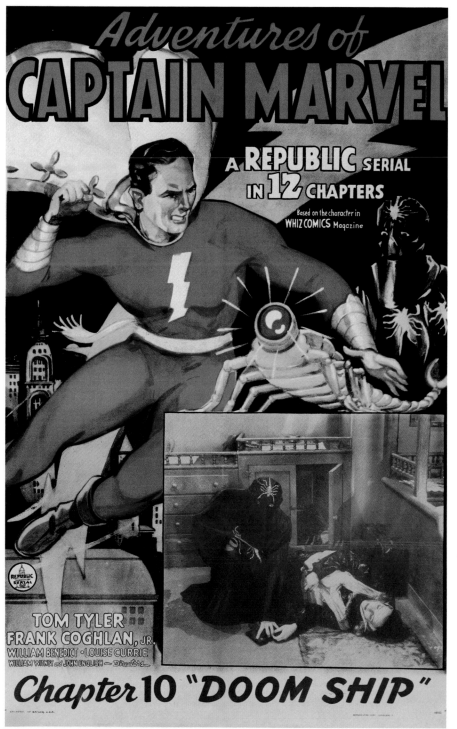

72. ADVENTURES OF CAPTAIN MARVEL,
Chapter 10, 1941, one-sheet

73. THE SPIDER RETURNS,
Chapter 2, 1941, one-sheet

74. DICK TRACY VS. CRIME INC.,
Chapter 1, 1941, one-sheet

75. DICK TRACY VS. CRIME INC.,
Chapter 2, 1941, one-sheet

76. JUNGLE GIRL,
Chapter 1, 1941, one-sheet

77. KING OF THE TEXAS RANGERS,
Chapter 1, 1941, one-sheet

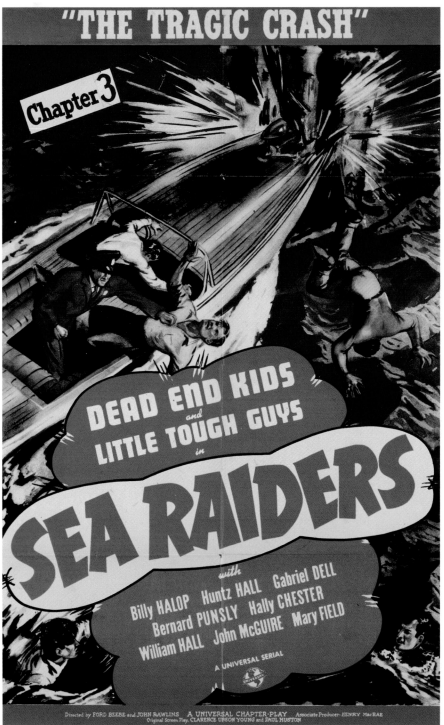

78. SEA RAIDERS,
Chapter 3, 1941, one-sheet

79. SKY RAIDERS,
entire serial, 1941, one-sheet

80. SPY SMASHER,
Chapter 12, 1942, one-sheet

81. CAPTAIN MIDNIGHT,
Chapter 6, 1942, one-sheet

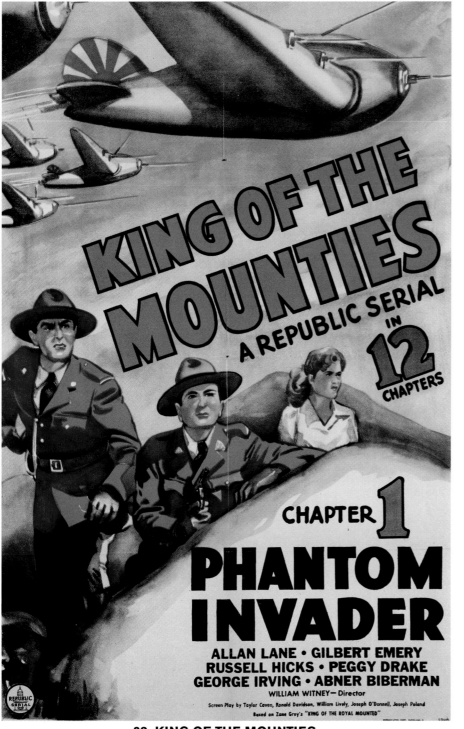

82. KING OF THE MOUNTIES,
Chapter 1, 1942, one-sheet

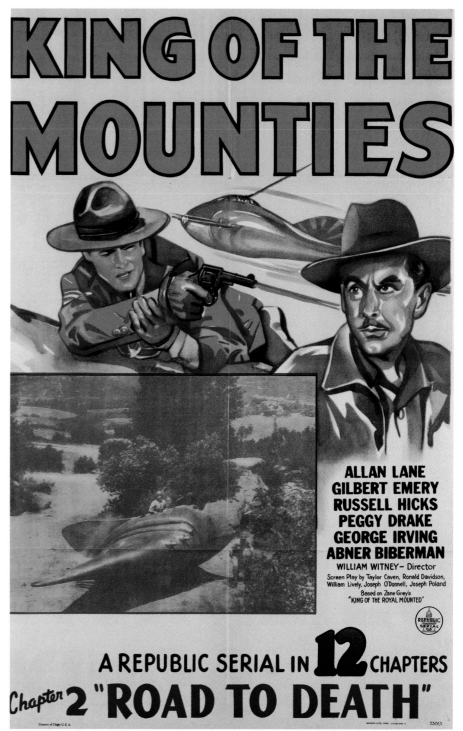

83. KING OF THE MOUNTIES,
Chapter 2, 1942, one-sheet

84. PERILS OF NYOKA,
Chapter 1, 1942, one-sheet

85. GANG BUSTERS,
entire serial, 1942, one-sheet

86. THE PHANTOM,
Chapter 12, 1943, one-sheet

87. THE BATMAN,
Chapter 1, 1943, one-sheet

88. DAREDEVILS OF THE WEST,
Chapter 1, 1943, one-sheet

89. DAREDEVILS OF THE WEST,
Chapter 4, 1943, one-sheet

90. G-MEN VS. THE BLACK DRAGON,
Chapter 1, 1943, one-sheet

91. G-MEN VS. THE BLACK DRAGON,
Chapter 5, 1943, one-sheet

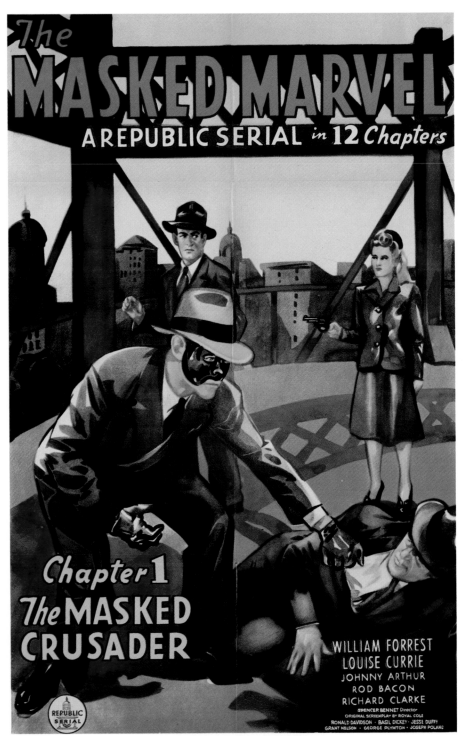

92. THE MASKED MARVEL,
Chapter 1, 1943, one-sheet

93. THE MASKED MARVEL,
Chapter 12, 1943, one-sheet

94. SECRET SERVICE IN DARKEST AFRICA,
Chapter 1, 1943, one-sheet

95. CAPTAIN AMERICA,
Chapter 1, 1944, one-sheet

96. THE TIGER WOMAN,
Chapter 1, 1944, one-sheet

97. THE TIGER WOMAN,
Chapter 12, 1944, one-sheet

98. ZORRO'S BLACK WHIP,
Chapter 1, 1944, one-sheet

99. ZORRO'S BLACK WHIP,
Chapter 12, 1944, one-sheet

100. MYSTERY OF THE RIVER BOAT,
entire serial, 1944, one-sheet

101. HAUNTED HARBOR,
Chapter 2, 1944, one-sheet

102. SECRET AGENT X-9,
entire serial, 1945, one-sheet

103. THE PURPLE MONSTER STRIKES,
entire serial, 1945, one-sheet

104. MANHUNT OF MYSTERY ISLAND,
Chapter 1, 1945, one-sheet

105. MANHUNT OF MYSTERY ISLAND,
Chapter 15, 1945, one-sheet

106. JUNGLE QUEEN,
entire serial, 1945, one-sheet

107. BRENDA STARR, REPORTER,
Chapter 9, 1945, one-sheet

108. THE ROYAL MOUNTED RIDES AGAIN,
entire serial, 1945, one-sheet

109. KING OF THE FOREST RANGERS,
entire serial, 1946, one-sheet

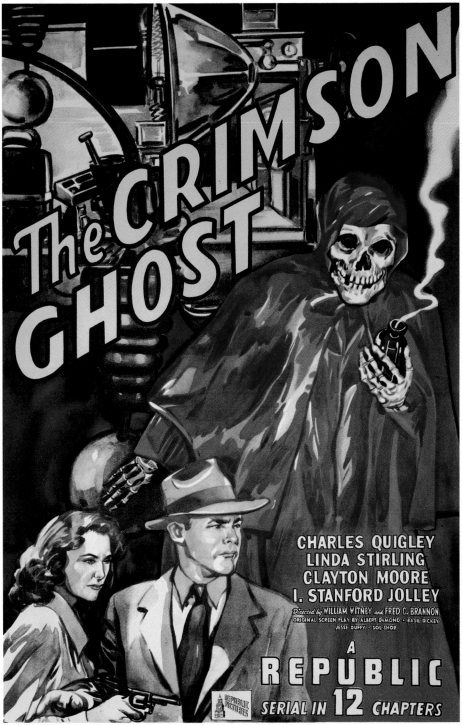

110. THE CRIMSON GHOST,
entire serial, 1946, one-sheet

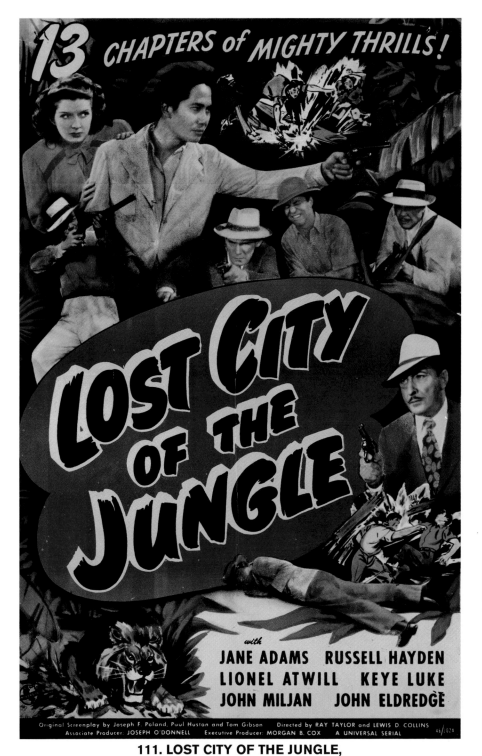

111. LOST CITY OF THE JUNGLE,
entire serial, 1946, one-sheet

112. BRICK BRADFORD,
Chapter 10, 1947, one-sheet

113. JESSE JAMES RIDES AGAIN,
entire serial, 1947, one-sheet

114. SUPERMAN,
Chapter 12, 1948, one-sheet

115. NEW ADVENTURES OF BATMAN & ROBIN,
Chapter 5, 1949, one-sheet

**116. NEW ADVENTURES OF
BATMAN AND ROBIN,**
Chapter 3, 1949, lobby cards

**117. NEW ADVENTURES OF
BATMAN AND ROBIN,**
Chapter 8, 1949, lobby cards

**118. NEW ADVENTURES OF
BATMAN AND ROBIN,**
Chapter 12, 1949, lobby cards

119. KING OF THE ROCKET MEN,
entire serial, 1949, one-sheet

120. LOST PLANET AIRMEN,
feature version of King of the Rocket Men, 1951, one-sheet

121. FEDERAL AGENTS VERSUS UNDERWORLD, INC.,
entire serial, 1949, one-sheet

122. ATOM MAN VS. SUPERMAN,
Chapter 9, 1950, one-sheet

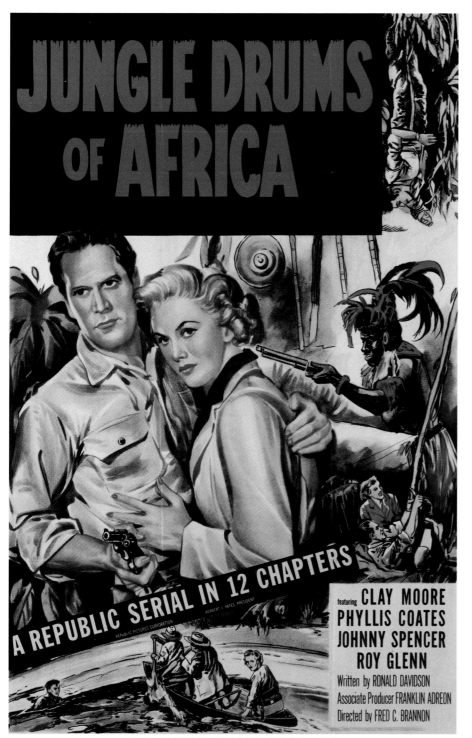

123. JUNGLE DRUMS OF AFRICA,
entire serial, 1952, one-sheet

124. COMMANDO CODY,
Chapter 1, 1953, one-sheet

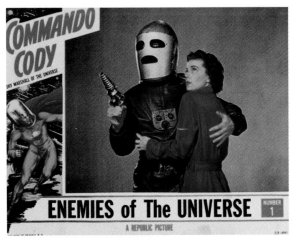

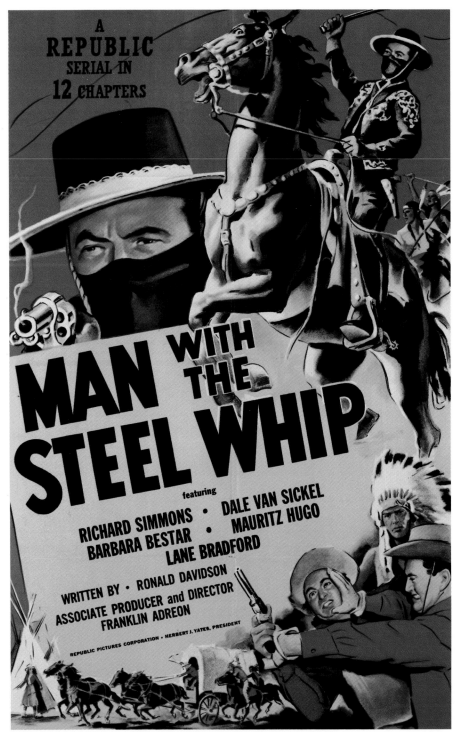

125. COMMANDO CODY,
4 Card Set, 1953, lobby cards

126. MAN WITH THE STEEL WHIP,
entire serial, 1954, one-sheet